JORDAN 2016 HUMAN RIGHTS REPORT

EXECUTIVE SUMMARY

The Hashemite Kingdom of Jordan is a constitutional monarchy ruled by King Abdullah II bin Hussein. The constitution concentrates executive and legislative authority in the king. The multiparty parliament consists of the 65-member House of Notables (Majlis al-Ayan) appointed by the king and a 130-member elected lower house, the Chamber of Deputies (Majlis al-Nuwwab). Elections for the Chamber of Deputies took place on September 20. International observers deemed the elections were organized, inclusive, and credible.

Civilian authorities maintained effective control over the security forces.

The most significant human rights problems were citizens' inability choose their ultimate governing authority; restrictions on the freedom of expression, including detention of journalists, which limited the ability of citizens and media to criticize government policies and officials; and mistreatment and allegations of torture by security and government officials.

Other human rights problems included restrictions on freedom of association and assembly, poor prison conditions, arbitrary arrest and denial of due process through administrative detention, prolonged detention, and allegations of nepotism and the influence of special interests on the judiciary. The government continued to infringe on citizens' privacy rights. The government prevented some refugees from coming into the country, deported other asylum seekers, and stripped some Palestinian refugees from Syria of their Jordanian citizenship prior to returning them involuntarily to Syria. Violence against women was widespread, and abuse of children persisted. Legal and societal discrimination and harassment remained a problem for women, religious minorities, religious converts, and lesbian, gay, bisexual, transgender, and intersex (LGBTI) persons. Trafficking in persons remained a problem. Discrimination against persons with disabilities was a problem. Legal and societal discrimination against persons of Palestinian origin remained widespread. The government restricted labor rights and local and international human rights organizations reported abuse of foreign domestic workers.

Impunity remained widespread, and the government did not take sufficiently strong steps to investigate, prosecute, or punish officials who committed abuses. The government took limited steps to investigate, prosecute, and punish officials who committed abuses, but the proceedings were not transparent, and information on the outcomes was not publicly available.

Section 1. Respect for the Integrity of the Person, Including Freedom from:

a. Arbitrary Deprivation of Life and other Unlawful or Politically Motivated Killings

There were some reports of arbitrary or unlawful deprivation of life. Local human rights organizations alleged that at least three individuals died in custody from torture during the year, but they did not publicly report specifics of the cases.

In April the National Coordinator for Human Rights announced that the police court was considering three cases of alleged torture by Public Security Directorate (PSD) personnel. The three police court cases, including the May 2015 death while in custody of Abduallah al-Zo'ubi and the September 2015 death while in custody of Omar al-Nasir, continued at year's end.

b. Disappearance

There were no reports during the year of politically motivated disappearances.

c. Torture and Other Cruel, Inhuman, or Degrading Treatment or Punishment

The constitution bans torture, including psychological harm, by public officials and provides penalties of as long as three years' imprisonment for its use, with a penalty of up to 15 years if serious injury occurs. While the law prohibits such practices, international and local nongovernmental organizations (NGOs) continued to report incidents of torture and widespread mistreatment in police and security detention centers. Human rights lawyers found the law ambiguous and supported amendments to define "torture" better and strengthen sentencing guidelines.

The police court case against five police officers charged with the torture of Omar al-Nasir continued. Omar al-Nasir died in custody at the Criminal Investigation Department's headquarters in Amman in late September 2015.

According to a report by the quasi-governmental National Center for Human Rights (NCHR), the PSD received and investigated 239 complaints of torture and mistreatment in police stations in 2015; 147 cases had no further action due to a decision by the police prosecutor, 45 were referred to the chief of a police unit for administrative punishment, and 27 remained pending. Authorities referred 20 complaints to the police court in comparison with one case in 2014. The NCHR received 92 complaints of torture and mistreatment in police stations in 2015.

The NCHR received complaints of torture and inhuman treatment, but did not report specifics of the allegations. Throughout the year a local NGO reported that, in an effort to humiliate detainees, government agents at times abused them during arrest or detention by making them remove their clothing and threatening them with rape. The NCHR reported in 2015 a sharp drop in complaints of torture and mistreatment at prisons and rehabilitation centers, while it observed an increase in complaints of torture and mistreatment against the Anti-Narcotics Department and the Criminal Investigation Department.

The 2015 NCHR report documented no effective steps by either the legislative or the executive powers to address torture and called for amending the law to give jurisdiction to ordinary courts to follow up on torture cases to ensure the trial and conviction of perpetrators of torture and that victims received compensation.

Prison and Detention Center Conditions

Conditions in the country's six older prisons were poor, while the eight new prisons met international standards. Authorities held migrants without legal work or residency permits, or charged with other crimes, in the same facilities as citizens. (For information on asylum seekers and refugees, see section 2.d.).

Physical Conditions: Significant problems in older prison facilities included inadequate health care, poor sanitation and ventilation, extreme temperatures, and insufficient basic and emergency medical care. In its 2015 report, the NCHR, identified as problems overcrowding; and limited health care, legal assistance for inmates, and social care for the inmates and their families. Detainees reported abuse and mistreatment by guards.

According to a report by the NCHR, in 2015 the PSD received 38 cases of allegations of torture and mistreatment in prisons and rehabilitation centers compared to 61 in 2014: authorities convicted 12 officers, but, in the other 30 cases, authorities took no further action for unspecified reasons. In 2015 the NCHR received eight complaints of torture and mistreatment at prisons and rehabilitation centers compared with 11 in 2014. According to NCHR there were

30 deaths in prisons in 2015, 26 of them were due to "natural causes," one was due to "unnatural causes" (beaten to death by a fellow inmate), and three were suicides.

Officials and the NCHR reported overcrowding at most of the prisons, especially the prisons in and around Amman. The NCHR repeatedly recommended the closure of Jweideh Prison, citing deteriorating infrastructure and inmates' complaints of poor social and medical care.

During the year the government closed eight temporary detention centers for failing to meet acceptable standards, and conducted renovations at an additional 17 temporary detention centers at police stations.

A 2014 law stipulates that juveniles and adult detainees should be held separately during the pretrial phases as well.

International and domestic NGOs reported that in some instances Islamist prisoners faced harsher prison conditions than other inmates.

Authorities often held pretrial detainees in the same detention facilities as convicted prisoners. The General Intelligence Directorate held some persons detained on national security charges in separate detention facilities. In 2015 the NCHR made an unspecified number of announced visits to directorate prisons, where the detainees complained of prolonged pretrial detention. The center received the following complaints about the Intelligence Directorate: solitary confinement and isolation of prisoners and prolonged detentions of up to one year. According to human rights activists and the 2015 NCHR report, the directorate held detainees in solitary confinement and did not allow unsupervised meetings with visitors, including their lawyers. There were also reports of mistreatment, abuse, and torture in their detention facilities. The 2015 NCHR report noted a decrease in the number of complaints related to the physical conditions of Intelligence Directorate detention facilities compared with previous years.

Although basic care was available in all correctional facilities, medical staff complained that correction facilities throughout the country lacked adequate facilities, supplies, and staff. The staff was unable to address deficiencies in care available to inmates. Most facilities were unable to conduct blood tests and had limited X-ray capabilities, forcing doctors to rely largely on patient self-reporting for certain conditions. If an inmate's condition was too severe for treatment at the clinic, doctors recommended transfer to a local hospital.

Conditions in the women's prison were generally better than conditions in most of the men's prison, but overcrowding at Jweideh was sometimes a problem.

<u>Administration</u>: During the year the PSD instituted a requirement that all temporary detention centers must keep a logbook recording the health status of each prisoner before and after detention. Authorities took no steps systematically to use alternatives to prison sentences for nonviolent offenders. As of 2014 the Juvenile Law recommends that judges use alternative sentencing, including community service and vocational training, for juveniles, although authorities had not done so. There were limited post-release programs and poor classification of inmates. Some newer prisons, such as Umm al-Lulu Prison, offered a range of vocational training programs and employment opportunities for adult male prisoners. There were no prison ombudsmen. In some cases authorities severely restricted the access of prisoners and detainees to visitors. In some cases authorities did not inform the families regarding the whereabouts of detainees and banned family visits. Prisoners could observe their religious practices. Authorities permitted prisoners and detainees to submit complaints to judicial authorities and, in some prisons, prison directors without censorship, but authorities rarely investigated allegations of poor conditions. Karamah, a team of government officials and NGOs, and the NCHR, a quasi-governmental organization, monitored prison conditions.

<u>Independent Monitoring</u>: The government permitted some local and international human rights observers to visit prisons and conduct private interviews. The International Committee of the Red Cross (ICRC) visited prisoners and detainees in all prisons, including those controlled by the Intelligence Directorate, according to standard ICRC modalities. Authorities denied requests by local human rights observers to conduct monitoring visits independently of Karamah and the NCHR. The prime minister-appointed national human rights coordinator organized monitoring visits for several local and international NGO representatives to the Jweideh Prison on January 21 and, after its renovation, on November 15. The coordinator organized a similar visit to Swaqah Prison on March 17.

<u>Improvements</u>: Early in the year, the government completed renovations of the men's section of Jweideh Prison to expand the living area for each inmate to meet international standards, including by installing fans in the rooms and toilets, and repairing the roof to prevent leaks. The renovations also created a new family visiting area, a dining hall, and an outdoor recreation area, renovated the mosque, clinic, and dentist's office, upgraded the sewage, electricity, heating, and water systems, and expanded the facility's capacity from 1,080 to 1,400.

d. Arbitrary Arrest or Detention

The law prohibits arbitrary arrest and detention; however, the government did not always observe these prohibitions.

Role of the Police and Security Apparatus

The PSD controls general police functions. The PSD, the Intelligence Directorate, the gendarmerie, the Civil Defense Directorate, and the military share responsibility for maintaining internal security. The PSD, the Civil Defense Directorate, and the gendarmerie report to the Minister of Interior with direct access to the king when necessary, and the Intelligence Directorate reports directly to the king. Civilian authorities maintained control over security forces.

According to local and international NGOs, the government rarely investigated allegations of abuse or corruption, and when authorities investigated such allegations, there were few convictions and little to no public information or transparency about the investigation and sentencing. Local and international NGOs and activists alleged widespread impunity. Citizens may file complaints of police abuse or corruption with the PSD's Ombudsman Bureau or at a police prosecutor stationed with each unit and at each prison. Citizens may file complaints of abuse and corruption by the gendarmerie directly with the PSD's Ombudsman Bureau. An Intelligence Directorate liaison officer receives complaints against the directorate and refers them to Intelligence Directorate personnel for investigation. Citizens may also file complaints against the PSD, gendarmerie, and the Intelligence Directorate with the NCHR, several human rights NGOs, or the civilian prosecutor general.

The PSD's Special Branch Unit is tasked with investigating allegations of police corruption. The PSD and the Intelligence Directorate try their personnel internally with their own courts, judges, and prosecutors; authorities rarely published reports about the proceedings. Trials rarely yielded substantive punishments for human rights violations, and authorities did not make such punishments public. Human rights activists cited fear of official retribution as a reason for the overall lack of official complaints of human rights violations.

Through June 30 the PSD Ombudsman Office had received eight complaints against officers that were allegations of harm (a lesser charge than torture that does not require a demonstration of intent). Authorities dismissed two cases for lack of evidence, and six remained pending. As of June 30, the PSD Ombudsman Office had received 32 other complaints against officers for disobeying the orders and instructions of a commander--such as an order to refrain from insulting inmates. Authorities dismissed four cases, and 28 remained pending.

The PSD includes a module on human rights in required annual training for all personnel. There is also a module on human rights in the required training for all new officers.

During the year there were few reported instances of security forces using excessive force with impunity and failing to protect demonstrators from violence. On June 13, a 14-year old boy died in Balqa Governorate during a police raid against suspected drug dealers. Police said the boy fell to his death as he ran from security forces. Two of the boys' relatives suggested in an online video that the police were responsible for the boy's death. The Public Security Directorate was investigating the incident. In 2015 the NCHR received 24 complaints concerning security personnel using excessive force during arrests and searches.

Arrest Procedures and Treatment of Detainees

The law allows authorities to detain suspects for up to 24 hours without a warrant in all cases. It requires that police notify authorities within 24 hours of an arrest and that authorities file formal charges within 15 days of an arrest. Authorities can extend the period to file formal charges to as long as six months for a felony and two months for a misdemeanor. According to local NGOs, prosecutors routinely requested extensions, which judges granted. The State Security Court authorizes judicial police to arrest and keep persons in custody for seven days prior to notification while conducting criminal investigations. This authority includes arrests for alleged misdemeanors. NGOs alleged that authorities transferred suspects to the State Security Court to extend the legal time from 24 hours to seven days for investigation prior to notification or transferred suspects from police station to police station to extend the period for investigation. The NCHR report criticized the lack of record keeping at police detention facilities, noting that records failed to note the exact time of arrest and the arresting employee.

The penal code allows bail, and authorities used it in some cases. Some detainees reported not having timely access to a lawyer or the ability to contact their relatives at the time of arrest, but authorities generally permitted family member visits, albeit sometimes up to a week after the arrest. Authorities appointed lawyers to represent indigent defendants charged with felonies carrying possible life sentences or the death penalty, although legal aid services remained minimal. The law provides the right to appear promptly before a judge or other judicial officer for a judicial determination of the legality of the detention. At times authorities held suspects incommunicado for up to one week or placed them under house arrest. A number of human rights activists alleged that authorities held arrestees incommunicado to hide evidence of physical abuse by security forces.

Arbitrary Arrest: In cases purportedly involving state security, security forces at times arrested and detained citizens in administrative detention without warrants or judicial review, held them in pretrial detention without informing them of the charges against them, and either did not allow defendants to meet with their lawyers or did not permit meetings until shortly before trial. Activists reported that, during the year, officials detained migrant laborers for working without authorization, being absent from their authorized workplace, or lacking proper residency permits. They reported employers physically abused or mistreated some of these detainees. On September 26, the Prisons Administration reported 1,058 persons were in administrative detention: 901 men and 157 women. In 2015 the NCHR reported 19,860 administrative detainees held throughout the year, some as long as five years.

The law allows the 12 provincial governors to detain administratively individuals suspected of planning to commit a crime or sheltering thieves, habitually stealing, or constituting a danger to the public. Authorities held these individuals in prison or house arrest without due process and often despite a finding of not guilty in legal proceedings. The governors may prolong detentions; authorities administratively detained some migrants for several months without charges. Governors used this provision widely, including to incarcerate women allegedly to protect them from becoming potential victims of honor crimes, although the detainees posed no threat to public safety.

Several international and national NGOs noted governors routinely abused the law, imprisoning individuals when there was not enough evidence to convict them and prolonging the detention of prisoners whose sentences had expired.

Pretrial Detention: The common practice of judges granting extensions to prosecutors prior to filing formal charges unnecessarily lengthened pretrial detention. Lengthy legal procedures, a large number of detainees, judicial inefficiency, and judicial backlog added to the problem of pretrial detention. Automation of several legal procedures in recent years reduced the average period of pretrial detention, according to local legal aid organizations.

The law criminalizes the act of detaining any person without a prosecutor's order for more than 24 hours. According to human rights organizations, impunity was very common for such violations.

Detainee's Ability to Challenge Lawfulness of Detention before a Court: The law does not have an explicit provision that entitles victims of arbitrary or unlawful detention to restitution. The Criminal Procedures Law does not provide for routine judicial review of administrative detentions ordered by the 12 governors. Detainees can bring civil lawsuits for restitution for arbitrary or unlawful detention or bring criminal lawsuits for illegal incarceration, but this rarely occurred in practice. Detainees must hire a lawyer with at least five years' experience, must pay their own fees, and must present a copy of the order of detention. In the only known case of compensation for unlawful detention, in 2015 the Court of Appeals upheld a 2014 decision by the Amman Magistrate Court to award compensation to an Egyptian worker for unlawful detention. Authorities had administratively detained the worker for 13 months.

e. Denial of Fair Public Trial

The law provides for an independent judiciary, but allegations of nepotism and the influence of special interests by legal experts and human rights lawyers raised concerns about the judiciary's independence. Additionally, judicial inefficiency and a large case backlog delayed the provision of justice. Authorities did not always respect court orders.

Trial Procedures

The law presumes that defendants are innocent. According to the law, all civilian court trials, as well as State Security Court trials are open to the public unless the court determines that the trial should be closed to protect the public interest. State Security Court trials are generally open to the journalists and NGOs, but the court can decide to close them if it deems it in the public interest. Authorities occasionally tried defendants in their absence. Defendants are entitled to legal counsel, provided at public expense for the indigent in cases involving the death penalty or life imprisonment, but only at the trial stage. Most criminal defendants lacked legal representation prior to and at trial. Officials did not respect the right of defendants to be informed promptly and in detail of the charges against them or to a fair and public trial without undue delay. Authorities did not uniformly provide foreign residents, especially foreign workers who often did not speak

Arabic, with translations and defense. Defendants may present witnesses and evidence and may question witnesses presented against them. Authorities generally granted defendants access to government-held evidence relevant to a case. Defendants can appeal verdicts; appeals are automatic for cases involving the death penalty. Defendants do not have the right to refuse to testify. Although the constitution prohibits the use of confessions extracted by torture, human rights activists noted that courts routinely accepted confessions allegedly extracted under torture or mistreatment.

Defendants before the State Security Court frequently met with their attorneys only one or two days before their trial began. Authorities did not accord defendants adequate time and facilities to prepare their defense. In many cases, the accused remained in detention without bail during the proceedings. In the State Security Court, defendants have the right to appeal their sentences to the Court of Cassation, which has the authority to review issues of both fact and law.

The government allowed international observers to visit the State Security Court and the Police Court to watch court proceedings in October 2015 and March. One of the cases observed at the police court in March was the trial of five police officials accused of torturing and beating Omar al-Nasir to death in September 2015. The case remained pending at year's end.

Civil, criminal, and commercial courts accord equal weight to the testimony of men and women. On the other hand, in sharia courts, which have jurisdiction over Muslim marriage, divorce, and inheritance cases, the testimony of one man equals that of two women.

Political Prisoners and Detainees

During the year the government detained and imprisoned activists for political reasons including criticizing the government, criticizing the government's foreign policy, the publication of criticism of government officials and official bodies, criticizing foreign countries, and chanting slogans against the king. Citizens and NGOs alleged the government continued to detain other individuals for political reasons and that governors continued to use administrative detention for what appeared to be political reasons.

On June 14, authorities detained Amjad Qourshah, a professor of religious studies at the University of Jordan. The State Security Court charged him with harming relations with a foreign state under the Counterterrorism Law. Qourshah said that the charges related to videos he published in 2014 criticizing the country's participation in the counter-Da'esh coalition. The State Security Court rejected six requests for bail from his lawyer before releasing him on bail on September 6. The charges were pending at year's end.

Civil Judicial Procedures and Remedies

Individuals may bring civil lawsuits related to human rights violations.

f. Arbitrary or Unlawful Interference with Privacy, Family, Home, or Correspondence

The law prohibits arbitrary interference in private matters, but the government did not respect this prohibition. Citizens widely believed that security officers monitored telephone conversations and internet communication, read private correspondence, and engaged in surveillance without court orders. Citizens widely believed the government employed an informer system within political movements and human rights organizations.

Activists reported that Intelligence Directorate officials withheld documents and threatened to bar children of activists from entering or graduating from university.

Former prisoners alleged authorities banned citizens from obtaining security clearances needed for employment.

Section 2. Respect for Civil Liberties, Including:

a. Freedom of Speech and Press

The constitution provides for freedom of speech and press, but the government did not respect these rights. Authorities applied articles of the Counterterrorism Law, the Cybercrimes Law, and the penal code to arrest local journalists.

Freedom of Speech and Expression: The law permits punishment of up to three years' imprisonment for insulting the king, slandering the government or foreign leaders, offending religious beliefs, or stirring sectarian strife and sedition. During the year the government restricted the ability of individuals to criticize the government by arresting a number of activists for political expression and for criticizing foreign governments. Authorities used laws against slander of public officials, blackmail, and libel to restrict public discussion, as well as employing official gag orders issued by the Media Commission.

On August 13, authorities arrested writer Nahed Hattar for posting an editorial cartoon on his Facebook page that included a personification of God. The prosecutor charged him with inciting sectarian strife and racism and insulting religion under the penal code. On September 8, authorities released him on bail. On September 25, a lone gunman shot and killed Hattar as he was entering the courthouse. Authorities detained the shooter. Hattar's family stated that Hattar and his lawyer had requested additional protection, which the government did not provide. The same day authorities reportedly identified 10 social media users that they intended to refer to the prosecutor general for spreading hate speech related to the cartoon and the shooting.

On September 22, authorities detained social media personality Zain Karazon on charges of slander and libel. Karazon has a following of more than one million on social media platform Snapchat. Reasons for her arrest were unclear at year's end. Some media sources speculated that a doctor or hospital sued her for criticizing a botched surgery, while other media sources suspected that someone had filed a suit related to a controversy involving a gay Lebanese online personality. On September 29, authorities released Karazon on bail. Charges were pending at year's end.

In January the State Security Court found Ali al-Malkawi guilty of insulting the king and sentenced him to six months' imprisonment. Since authorities had already detained al-Malkawi for six months, authorities sentenced him to time served and released him immediately after sentencing. Authorities had arrested al-Malkawi in July 2015 for a posting on his Facebook page criticizing Arab and Islamic inaction in protecting Burmese Muslims.

All public-opinion polls and survey research require authorization from the Bureau of Statistics, although the law was not enforced. NGOs stated that the measure could be enforced, even retroactively, and called for the government to rescind it.

Press and Media Freedoms: Independent print media existed, including several major daily newspapers, although such publications must obtain licenses from the state to operate. The independent print and broadcast media largely operated with limited restriction, and media observers reported government pressure, including the threat of large fines and prison sentences, to refrain from criticizing the royal family, discussing the Intelligence Directorate, using language deemed offensive to religion, or slandering government officials. The government influenced news reporting and commentary through political pressure on editors and control over important editorial positions in government-affiliated media. Journalists of government-affiliated and independent media reported that security officials attempted to influence reporting and place articles favorable to the government through bribes, threats, and political pressure.

The Audiovisual Law grants the head of the Media Commission the authority to close any unlicensed theater, satellite channel, or radio channel. The Media Commission cannot grant a new broadcasting license to a company unless all shares are Jordanian-owned. Additionally, those with licenses should not broadcast anything that would harm public order, social security, the economy, national security, or Jordan's relations with a foreign country; incite hatred, terrorism, violent sedition; or mislead or deceive the public. There is a fine for broadcasting without a license. The cabinet, however, must justify the reasons for rejecting a license and allow the applicant to appeal the decision to the judiciary.

Authorities arrested or temporarily detained some journalists, and government officials or private individuals threatened some journalists.

On February 14, authorities arrested *al-Ra'i* journalist Zaid Murafai for publishing an article on a protest by judges and court employees regarding losses in their pension fund. The court charged Murafai with slander and defamation under the Cybercrimes Law, as well as reporting on a pending case. Authorities released Murafai on bail four days later; charges remained pending at year's end.

The government has a majority of seats on the board for the leading semiofficial daily newspaper, *al-Rai*, and a share of board seats for *ad-Dustour* daily newspaper. According to press freedom advocates, the Intelligence Directorate's Media Department must approve editors in chief of progovernment newspapers.

Media observers noted that, when covering controversial subjects, government-owned Jordan Television, Jordan News Agency, and Radio Jordan reported only the government's position.

By law any book can be published and distributed freely. If, however, the Press and Publications Directorate deems passages religiously offensive or "insulting" to the king, it can request a court order to prohibit the distribution of the book.

Violence and Harassment: The government subjected journalists to harassment and intimidation.

In its 2015 semiannual report *Media Freedom in the Arab World*, the Center for Defending the Freedom of Journalists documented 15 incidents of serious violations against journalists in the country in 2015: 10 detentions, two cases of physical assault, two cases of humiliating treatment, and one injury.

The center documented 50 violations against 28 journalists covering the September 20 parliamentary elections. Violations included cases of poll workers obstructing journalists' work, withholding information, and preventing photography. There was once case of deleting photographs from a camera.

On February 22, private television station Ro'ya News wrote that security officials beat and arrested one of their journalists who had been covering a protest in front of parliament.

Censorship or Content Restrictions: The government directly and indirectly censored the media. Journalists claimed that the government used informants in newsrooms and exercised influence over reporting and that Intelligence Directorate officials censored reporting. Editors reportedly received telephone calls from security officials instructing them how to cover events or to refrain from covering certain topics or events, especially criticism of political reform. Bribery of journalists took place and undermined independent reporting. On occasion, government officials provided texts for journalists to publish under their bylines. Journalists reported self-censorship due to the threat of detention and imprisonment for defamation for a variety of offenses and court-ordered compensation of as much as 150,000 Jordanian Dollars (JD) ($210,000). At times, editors in chief censored articles to prevent lawsuits. The government's use of "soft containment" of journalists, including the withholding of financial support, scholarships for relatives, and special invitations, led to significant control of media content.

During the year the Media Commission issued several gag orders restricting discussion of certain topics in all forms of media, including social media. For example, the government issued gag orders restricting discussion of the court cases against Amjad Qourshah and Nahed Hattar, as well as the shooting of Nahed Hattar.

The annual report of the Center for Defending Freedom of Journalists noted that 93 percent of journalists surveyed in 2015 said they practiced self-censorship.

The government continued to enforce bans on the distribution of selected books for religious, moral, and political reasons. The Media Commission banned 41 books during the year for violating public norms and values (such as by including sexual content), disrespecting religion, or insulting the king.

Libel/Slander Laws: Government prosecutors relied on privately initiated libel, slander, and defamation lawsuits to suppress criticism. Dozens of journalists, as well as members of parliament, faced libel and slander accusations filed by private citizens.

On January 5, authorities charged comedian Omar Zorba with slander and defamation under the Cybercrimes Law for criticizing a song that aired on the official television station promoting the national census. The presenter who hosted the segment filed the suit. Charges remained pending at year's end.

On May 17, authorities arrested and detained *ad-Dustour* journalist Anas Sweileh for publishing an article on an abandoned building used by unemployed youth for repeated threats of suicide. The owner of the building filed a complaint. The court charged Sweileh with slander, defamation, and libel. Authorities released Sweileh on bail the same day; charges remained pending at year's end.

National Security: The government used laws protecting national security to restrict criticism of government policies and officials. The government also issued gag orders restricting discussion on all forms of media after a fatal shooting by a lone gunman at an Intelligence Directorate office in Balqa on June 6 and a suicide bombing against a northeast border installation on June 21.

Internet Freedom

There were government restrictions on access to the internet. The law requires the licensing and registration of online news websites, holds editors responsible for readers' comments on their websites, requires that website owners provide the government with the personal data of its users, and mandates that editors in chief be members of the Jordan Press Association. The law gives authorities explicit power to block and censor websites. Authorities blocked a news website for one week in August for a licensing issue. The website published a statement saying that the block was under a false legal pretext, and that some governmental and regulatory bodies were critical of the website's having published articles attacking the mufti and the media commission.

The registration fee for a news website is 1,400 JD ($1,960). The owner and editor in chief can be fined between 3,000 JD ($4,200) and 5,000 JD ($7,000), in addition to criminal penalties, for website content that "includes humiliation, defamation, or disparaging individuals in a manner that violates their personal freedoms or spreads false rumors about them."

According to journalists, security forces reportedly demanded websites remove some posted articles. The government threatened websites and journalists that criticized the government, while it actively supported those that reported favorably on the government. The government monitored electronic correspondence and internet chat sites. Individuals believed they were unable to express their views fully or freely via the internet, including by personal e-mail.

According to UNESCO's Media Development Indicators published in September 2015, internet penetration was 76 percent during the year, up from 38 percent in 2010.

Academic Freedom and Cultural Events

The government placed some limits on academic freedom. Some members of the academic community claimed there was a continuing intelligence presence in academic institutions, including monitoring academic conferences and lectures. The government monitored political meetings, speech on university campuses, and sermons in mosques and churches. Academics reported the Intelligence Directorate must clear all university professors before their appointment and that the university administration must approve all research papers, forums, reading materials, movies, or seminars, which in turn clears potentially controversial material through the Intelligence Directorate. Authorities edit commercial foreign films for sexual content before screening in commercial theaters.

On April 26, the government withdrew authorization for a planned concert by Mashrou' Leila, a Lebanese alternative rock band. The Ministry of Tourism stated that the performance would have been at odds with the "authenticity" of the venue, a historic amphitheater. The band wrote that authorities unofficially told them that their political and religious beliefs were at odds with the country's customs and traditions.

b. Freedom of Peaceful Assembly and Association

Freedom of Assembly

The constitution provides for freedom of assembly, but the government limited this right. Security forces generally permitted demonstrations and provided security at announced demonstrations.

On February 21, security forces disrupted a demonstration in front of parliament organized by several political parties against the draft elections law. Two female members of parliament participating in the protest accused security forces of using excessive force. Authorities arrested and later released three protesters who refused to disperse and one journalist covering the event. Security officials stated that the protesters did not have approval for the demonstration.

On June 22, authorities used force to disperse an eight-week-long protest in the central town of Dhiban. Eighteen unemployed youths demanded government assistance in finding employment. Gendarmerie used tear gas to disperse the protesters and removed a tent the protesters had erected. In response, several protesters threw rocks, burned tires, fired in the air, and chanted slogans against the government. Authorities arrested more than 30 individuals for throwing stones at security forces but released the majority at dawn the next day. The government detained three individuals for attempted murder, resisting arrest, firing live ammunition in the air, and insulting the king. Authorities released two on bail on July 17 and the third on July 29. Charges were pending at year's end.

Several local and international NGOs reported that hotels required them to present letters of approval from the governor prior to holding training, private meetings, or public conferences. The government denied authorization for several events. Without letters of approval from the government and security services, hotels cancelled the events and trainings. In some cases NGOs relocated the events and training to private offices. Authorities denied permission to the Jordanian Muslim Brotherhood association (which is not legally registered as an association or NGO by the government) and the Islamic Action Front (legally registered as a political party) to hold meetings and events on several occasions throughout the country.

Freedom of Association

The constitution provides for the right of association, but the government limited this freedom. The law authorizes the Ministry of Social Development to reject applications to register an organization or to permit any organization to receive foreign funding for any reason. It prohibits the use of associations for the benefit of any political organization. The law also gives the ministry significant control over the internal management of associations, including the ability to dissolve associations, appoint new boards of directors, send government representatives to any board meeting, prevent associations from merging their operations, and appoint an auditor to examine an association's finances for any reason. The law requires associations to inform the ministry of board meetings, submit all board decisions for approval, disclose members' names, and obtain security clearances for board members from the Interior Ministry. The law includes penalties, including fines up to 10,000 JD ($14,000), for violations of the regulations. During 2015 the Ministry of Social Development introduced an application form for the approval process for associations that receive foreign funding. Associations criticized the procedure, which incorporated additional ministries into the decision process and removed the deadline for review of funding requests.

During the year NGOs reported that the government sometimes rejected requests for foreign funding, whereas such rejections were previously extremely rare. As of August 25, the ministry had received 250 applications for foreign funding. The government approved 170 applications, denied 10, and requested additional documentation for five applications. Sixty-five applications remained "under consideration." NGO contacts reported that unexplained, months-long delays in the decision process increased significantly.

As of April the ministry registered 40 NGOs, dissolved 65, and warned 50. Authorities dissolved NGOs for violating the Associations Law.

Citizens widely suspected that the government infiltrated civil society organizations, political parties, and human rights organizations and their internal meetings.

c. Freedom of Religion

See the Department of State's *International Religious Freedom Report* at www.state.gov/religiousfreedomreport/.

d. Freedom of Movement, Internally Displaced Persons, Protection of Refugees, and Stateless Persons

The law provides for freedom of internal movement, foreign travel, emigration, and repatriation, although there were some restrictions. The United Nations reported that the government generally cooperated with the Office of the UN High Commissioner for Refugees (UNHCR), the UN Relief and Works Agency for Palestine Refugees in the Near East (UNRWA), and humanitarian organizations in providing protection and assistance to internally displaced persons, refugees, returning refugees, asylum seekers, stateless persons, and other persons of concern.

<u>In-country Movement</u>: The government placed some restrictions on the free internal movement of registered Syrian refugees and Syrian asylum seekers. From March 9 to June 21, the government admitted 21,300 vulnerable Syrian asylum seekers from the northeastern border where tens of thousands of Syrians had begun to gather along the Jordanian border. There were no reliable estimates as to what percentage of the population at the border were asylum seekers: UNHCR and the government agreed that the population included genuine asylum seekers, those wanting to remain in Syria but seeking safety from aerial bombardment, traffickers, smugglers, and armed actors. The government accommodated the admitted asylum seekers in a fenced-off section of Azraq camp pending additional security screening, as many had fled from Da'esh-controlled areas. Prior to June 21, authorities cleared approximately 5,000 persons and transferred them from the fenced-off section. Since June 21, after a suicide attack at a border crossing killed seven members of the Jordanian border guard force, approximately 16,000 refugees remained in the secured section of the camp, where they have restricted or limited access to health, education, psychosocial, and other services available in the rest of the camp. Authorities have cleared approximately 1,000 persons and transferred them since June 21. Authorities removed 201 from the camp and returned them to Syria. Similarly, since June 21, authorities have detained at Ruweishid transit center 380 Syrian asylum seekers who were in the process of transfer to Azraq camp when the suicide attack occurred and who continued to receive basic humanitarian assistance.

Authorities continued to subject Palestinian refugees from Syria held at Cyber City, a refugee camp in a closed government facility in Ramtha, to strict controls on their ability to leave the facility. Authorities allowed Palestinian residents of Cyber City to visit their relatives once per month, for two to three days at a time. Authorities made some exceptions for the sick and elderly to allow twice-monthly visits. Unlike Syrian refugees at Cyber City, Palestinian refugees were not entitled to the bailout system of a Jordanian guarantor. Authorities did not officially inform Palestinian refugees of the reasons for their restricted movement. On October 17, the government closed Cyber City and moved remaining residents to

King Abdullah Park. Restrictions on movement of Palestinian refugees from Syria remained in place at King Abdullah Park.

Foreign Travel: Former prisoners and the 2015 NCHR report alleged authorities withheld passports and imposed travel bans against citizens.

Protection of Refugees

Access to Asylum: As of November 9, the government, in cooperation with UNHCR, reported more than 655,000 registered Syrian refugees, and hundreds of thousands of additional nonrefugee Syrians in the country. Additionally, UNHCR registered more than 70,000 other refugees or asylum seekers in the country.

The country's laws do not provide for the granting of asylum or refugee status, and the government lacked a formal system of protecting refugees. Although it is not a signatory to the 1951 Convention Relating to the Status of Refugees or its 1967 Protocol, the government respected UNHCR's eligibility determinations regarding asylum seekers, including those who entered the country illegally. A 1998 memorandum of understanding between the government and UNHCR, renewed in 2014, contains the definition of a refugee, confirms adherence to the principle of nonrefoulement, and allows recognized refugees a maximum stay of one year, during which period UNHCR must find a durable solution. The time limit is renewable, and, generally, the government did not force refugees to return to their country of origin. As of 2014 authorities required all Syrians in the country to obtain an official residency card from the Ministry of Interior. Among the requirements to obtain the new residency card, all Syrians over the age of 12 must obtain an individual health certificate, which costs five JD (seven dollars).

The government continued to limit the number of Syrians seeking asylum in the country, as well as the points of entry they may use. Generally, the government restricted entry of Syrians by air despite formal visa-free travel between the countries. Authorities did not allow Syrian asylum seekers, except severe medical cases, to enter along the more populated northwest border of the country. Instead, authorities allowed Syrian refugees seeking entry to cross only at one of the two informal borders crossings along the northeast desert border. The government limited the numbers of new arrivals on a daily basis between January and March. In March the government expedited the entry of 21,300 additional refugees at this informal border point between March and June but limited other refugees from crossing at these informal points. Since June 21, after a suicide attack at a border crossing killed seven Jordanian border guards, the government closed the border and declared the surrounding area a "closed military zone." The government has restricted humanitarian access to the area. Based on Jordanian estimates, international organizations reported that between 70,000 and 100,000 Syrians camped at the northeast desert Jordan-Syria border throughout the year. Several international organizations, including UNHCR, publicly called on the government to grant entry to the asylum seekers, especially the sick, elderly, children, and pregnant women, many of whom had waited in the border area for months in substandard shelters, with limited food and water, and most without medical care. From August 2 to 4, the government allowed international organizations to deliver a one-month food ration across the border and to continue to deliver water daily. Other refugees, including many Iraqis and Yemenis, faced questioning at formal entry points, and authorities refused entry to many of them. The government's 2013 announcement that it would not allow entry into Jordan of Palestinian refugees from Syria remained in effect throughout the year.

Refoulement: The government forcibly returned Syrian refugees and Palestinian refugees from Syria, including women, children, war-injured, and persons with disabilities to Syria. International organizations reported that the government carried out a preliminary screening of refugees waiting at the northeastern border and prevented some Syrians seeking refuge from entering the country. International organizations also reported that the government forcibly returned to Syria some refugees residing in Azraq camp and Ruwaished transit center after authorities had admitted them for additional screening via the informal border crossings in the northeast.

The government also returned to Syria some Syrian refugees found working illegally, living in informal tented settlements, or not presenting refugee documentation when moving internally, while forcing others to return to formal refugee camps. Authorities most often sent those subjected to refoulement to Dara'a Province, where many had no support network or way to return across battle lines to their homes, which were often within regime- or Da'esh-controlled areas.

Through September, the UNRWA was aware of 24 cases of refoulement of Palestinian refugees from Syria. The vulnerability of Palestinian refugees from Syria to deportation increased their risk of other abuses. For those who entered the country irregularly (without required documentation, or using Syrian identity documents), refoulement was a constant risk, and access to basic civil services-- including renewal of identity documents, the registration of marriages, deaths, and births--was highly complex. The UNRWA reported that such activities could result in forced return to Syria, as well as detention and denaturalization.

Employment: In February the government announced it would allow Syrian refugees access to the formal labor market and committed to providing 50,000 opportunities for Syrians during the year. The Ministry of Labor issued nearly 32,000 work permits to Syrians between February and November. The government took several steps to expand and facilitate work permit issuance, including waiving fees and offering extended amnesties for those working illegally to regularize status. The government also revised work permit practices to allow Syrian workers in the agricultural sector to switch employers under the supervision of agricultural cooperatives, rather than requiring new work permits for each job transfer.

There have been some delays in implementing the new procedures at Ministry of Labor offices in governorates outside Amman, uncertainty among the refugee population on how to apply for the work permits, or whether they would lose eligibility to UNHCR assistance if they entered the legal workplace. Tens of thousands of Syrian refugees continued to work in the informal economy. A government-commissioned study report on migrant workers published in July estimated that 26 percent of Syrian refugees are economically active in the Jordan labor market. Very few non-Syrian refugees had access to the formal labor market and because of the difficulties and expenses involved in seeking work authorization, many worked in the unofficial labor market. Through September 18, the Ministry of Labor reported apprehending nearly 13,000 illegal foreign workers, 3,000 of whom were Syrians. There were reports of administrative detentions and deportations of Syrian refugees for working without authorization, as well as reports of Syrian refugees forcibly moved from their areas of employment into one of the refugee camps for working without authorization.

Longstanding Palestinian refugees with Jordanian identity documents were well integrated into the Jordanian workforce. This was not the case, however, for the approximately 158,000 Palestinian refugees originally from Gaza, who were not eligible for Jordanian citizenship and were unable to work legally or access public services. Additionally, according to UNRWA, authorities deprived Palestinian refugees from Syria, the majority of whom were without Jordanian documents, of the opportunity to work.

Access to Basic Services: The government generally transported Syrian refugees who arrived at informal border crossings and whom authorities admitted to the country to Raba'a Sarhan reception center. Most were registered with the government; received food, water, and medical attention from UNHCR and the ICRC; and were transported by the International Organization for Migration to a refugee camp. Since 2014, authorities have limited entry to Syrians seeking access to asylum along the northeastern border. Although numbers fluctuated, international organizations reported, based on Jordanian estimates, that 70,000 to 100,000 Syrians camped at the northeast desert Jordan-Syria border throughout the year. An undetermined number were inside the country beyond an earthen berm in harsh desert conditions, and tens of thousands resided on the Syrian side of the border. Prior to the border closure on June 21, these Syrians had adequate food and water provided by international organizations but health and hygiene conditions were inadequate as was access to medical aid and shelter. After the border closure on June 21, humanitarian organizations did not have access to the population. Water deliveries continued, but organizations only made one delivery of a 30-day supply of food on August 2 to 4. Authorities did not permit the stranded population to enter Jordan or register as refugees. Authorities permitted some international organizations to visit or assess the situation of these refugees, although not regularly, and very rarely after June 21.

The government excluded Palestinian refugees from Gaza who entered the country following the 1967 war from services otherwise available to Palestinian refugees, such as access to public assistance or public medical services. They were eligible to receive UNRWA services.

As of August 31, 16,661 Palestinian refugees from Syria had recorded their presence in country with the UNRWA.

The government allowed Syrian and other UNHCR-registered refugees to access public health and education facilities. Since 2014, authorities have charged Syrian refugees for health care at the same rates as uninsured Jordanians, who pay a nominal fee for most basic health services. Iraqi and other refugees must pay the foreigner's rate for health care. The government continued to provide free primary and secondary education to Syrian refugee children, and the minister of education announced that all school-age Syrian refugees should have access to education by the end of the year. Non-Syrian refugees must pay to attend government schools. Public schools, particularly in the north of the country, were overcrowded and operated on a double-shift schedule to accommodate the high number of students. The government doubled the number of double-shift schools to allow an additional 50,000 Syrian refugee students access to formal education on top of the 145,000 enrolled last year. For those not eligible to access formal education, because they have been out of school for three years or more, the Ministry of Education is developing a catch-up program to reach another 25,000 students between the ages of nine and 12. As of November preliminary Ministry of Education enrollment data indicated authorities had enrolled 165,000 Syrian refugees in schools whereas authorities registered approximately 1,200 Syrian schoolchildren for the catch-up classes. Children over the age of 12 who are not eligible to enroll in formal education could participate in a Ministry of Education-run nonformal education dropout program. These three initiatives extend educational opportunities to nearly all school-aged Syrian refugees. Refugees had equal access to justice regardless of their legal status, but did not always exercise this right.

Temporary Protection: The government also provided temporary protection to individuals who may not qualify as refugees. As of November 9, there were 655,716 Syrian refugees, registered by the government and UNHCR. As of November there were 60,067 Iraqi refugees and asylum seekers registered with UNHCR. The government tolerated the prolonged stay of many Iraqis and other refugees beyond the expiration of the visit permits under which they had entered the country. As of November 9, there were 5,096 Yemenis, 3,222 Sudanese, 775 Somalis, and 1,375 other populations registered with UNHCR and resident in Jordan.

Stateless Persons

Only the father can transmit citizenship. Women do not have the legal right to transmit citizenship to their children. Children of female citizens married to noncitizen husbands receive the nationality of the father and lose the right to attend public school or seek other government services if they do not hold legal residency, for which they must apply every year, and authorities do not assure continued residency. In guidelines announced by the government in 2014, if children of Jordanian mothers and noncitizen fathers apply and meet certain criteria, they may gain access to certain services enjoyed by citizens, including access to free primary and secondary education and subsidized health care; the ability to own property, invest, obtain a Jordanian driver's license; and have employment priority over other foreigners. The minister of interior stated that this ruling affected 88,983 families, including 355,932 children, in which the father lacked Jordanian citizenship. An estimated 55,000 of these fathers were of Palestinian origin. To access these services, children must obtain a special identification card through the Civil Status Bureau. To qualify, applicants must prove the maternal relationship, that the Jordanian mother has been resident in Jordan for five years, and that the children currently reside in Jordan. In April the

Civil Status Bureau began issuing identification cards to replace the initial certificates. By law the cabinet may approve citizenship for children of Jordanian mothers and foreign fathers, but this mechanism was not widely known, and approval rarely occurred.

Women may not petition for citizenship for noncitizen husbands, who may apply for citizenship only after fulfilling a requirement of 15 years' continuous residency. Once a husband has obtained citizenship, he may apply to transmit citizenship to his children. Such an application could take years, and the government could deny the application. Activists did not identify any obstacles standing in the way of naturalization for men who fulfilled this residency requirement.

Syrian refugees were sometimes unable to obtain birth certificates for children born in the country if they could not present an official marriage certificate or other nationality documents, which were sometimes lost or destroyed when they fled, or government authorities confiscated them when the refugees entered the country. Refugee households headed by women faced difficulty in certifying nationality of offspring in absence of the father, which increased the risk of statelessness among this population. Authorities established civil registry departments and sharia courts in the Za'atri and Azraq camps to help refugees register births.

Section 3. Freedom to Participate in the Political Process

The law does not provide citizens the ability to choose their ultimate governing authority. The king appoints and dismisses the prime minister, cabinet, and the upper house of parliament; dissolves parliament; and directs major public policy initiatives. Citizens have the ability to choose the lower house of parliament in generally credible periodic elections based on universal and equal suffrage and conducted by secret ballot. Citizens also elect most mayors and members of municipal councils. The cabinet, based on the prime minister's recommendations, appoints the mayors of Amman, Wadi Musa (Petra), and Aqaba, a special economic zone. Elections for the lower house of parliament took place on September 20. Elections for mayors and municipal councils took place in 2013.

Elections and Political Participation

Recent Elections: On September 20, the government held parliamentary elections administered by the Independent Electoral Commission. The commission is an autonomous legal entity. It supervises and administers all phases of parliamentary elections and municipal elections, as well as other elections called for by the Council of Ministers. Local and international monitors noted the elections were generally credible and technically well administered. The commission instituted several changes to the election process: it used preprinted and standardized ballots with numerous security features, created a website to respond to public queries, instituted an automated text message response to inquiries about polling stations, and held videos and workshops to familiarize the public with the electoral process.

The elections took place under a new electoral law, passed by parliament and ratified by the king on March 13. The new electoral law establishes an open-list proportional electoral system. The election exhibited important technical advances in administration, but observers cited allegations of vote buying, ballot box tampering in one region, and other concerns. International and domestic observers of the election process expressed reservations about inadequacies in the electoral legal framework and stressed the need to allocate seats to districts proportionally based on population size.

Several Islamist parties participated in the September 20 parliamentary election, ending a six-year boycott. The Islamic Action Front lists won 15 seats, including 10 for party members, while other Islamist candidates and parties won at least 12 seats.

The government held municipal elections in 2013. The Ministry of Municipal Affairs administered the elections, while the commission, which at the time did not have the authority to run municipal elections, played an advisory and monitoring role. During the municipal elections, civil society election monitors reported several irregularities and incidents of violence. In 2014, parliament passed a constitutional amendment to broaden the mandate of the commission to oversee municipal elections.

<u>Political Parties and Political Participation</u>: The Political Parties Law places supervisory authority of political parties in the Ministry of Political and Parliamentary Affairs. Political parties must have 150 founding members, all of whom must be citizens habitually resident in the country and not be a member of another non-Jordanian political organization, a judge, or affiliated with the security services. There is no quota for women when founding a new political party. Parties may not be formed on the basis of religion, sect, race, gender, or origin. The law stipulates citizens may not be prosecuted for their political party affiliation. The Committee on Political Party Affairs oversees the activities of political parties. The secretary general of the Ministry of Political and

Parliamentary Affairs chairs the committee, which includes a representative from the Ministry of Interior, the Ministry of Justice, the Ministry of Culture, the NCHR, and civil society. The law grants the committee the authority to approve or reject applications to establish or dissolve parties. It allows party founders to appeal a rejection to the judiciary within 60 days of the decision. According to the law, approved parties can only be dissolved subject to the party's own bylaws, or by a judicial decision for affiliation with a foreign entity, accepting funding from a foreign entity, violating provisions of the law, or violating provisions of the constitution. In March parliament approved the bylaw on government funding for political parties. The bylaw stipulated 50,000 JD ($70,000) annual financial support to political parties older than one year with more than 500 members from seven governorates, at least 10 percent of whom are women. The law also included additional financial support for parties that join coalitions of at least 12 parties; win at least one seat in parliament; and open additional branches beyond the minimum of a headquarter and four branch offices. The law prohibits membership in unlicensed political parties. There were 50 registered political parties, but they were weak, generally had vague platforms, and were personality centered. The strongest and most organized political party was the Islamic Action Front.

In December 2015 the king ratified the Decentralization Law that establishes two councils to participate in the budgeting process at the governorate level: the Governorates' Council will be 85 percent elected and 15 percent appointed, and the Executive Council fully appointed. The appointed council will be composed of technical experts from the central government. The majority-elected council has a 15 percent quota for women (10 percent elected and 5 percent appointed).

<u>Participation of Women and Minorities</u>: There are no laws limiting the participation of women and minorities in the political process, and they participated. The electoral law limits the parliamentary representation of certain minorities to designated quota seats. Human rights activists, however, cited cultural bias against women as an impediment to women participating in political life on the same scale as men. There is an 11.5 percent (15 seats) quota for women in the lower house of parliament and a 25 percent (243 seats) quota for women in municipal councils. In the parliamentary elections, voters elected 20 women to the lower house, five of whom won by outright competition outside the quota. The king appointed 10 female members to the upper house. Appointed on September 28, the 30-member cabinet included two female ministers: the minister of information and communications technology and public sector development; and the minister of tourism and antiquities. In the municipal elections, regulations

allocated women 297 out of 970 municipal council seats (30 percent). The Municipalities Law includes a 25-percent quota for women for municipal council seats. The Decentralization Law includes a 15-percent quota for women on the elected governorate councils.

Citizens of Palestinian origin were underrepresented at all levels of government and the military. The law reserves nine seats in the lower house of parliament for Christians and three seats for the Circassian and Chechen ethnic minorities combined, constituting an overrepresentation of these minorities. In the parliamentary elections, nine Christians won seats, one of them on the national list that is open to all religions and ethnicities. The law stipulates that Muslims must hold all parliamentary seats not specifically reserved for Christians or on the national list. There were five Christians in the upper house of parliament. There are no reserved seats for the relatively small Druze population, but its members may hold office under their government classification as Muslims. Christians served as cabinet ministers and ambassadors. There were three Christian ministers in the cabinet. Muslims held all senior command positions in the armed forces as of September. In recent years few Christians remained in the military long enough to reach senior command positions, leaving for more lucrative private-sector jobs, according to Christian former military officers.

Section 4. Corruption and Lack of Transparency in Government

The law provides criminal penalties for official corruption, although the government did not implement the law effectively. Officials often engaged in corrupt practices with impunity. During the year there were some investigations into allegations of corruption but very few convictions. The use of family, business, and other personal connections to advance personal business interests was widespread. There were allegations of lack of transparency in government procurement, government appointments, and dispute settlement.

In May the king ratified a new anticorruption law that merged the Anti-Corruption Commission and the Ombudsman Bureau into the new National Integrity Center to promote efficiencies and reduce duplication. Parliament passed the law in April. The law shortened the statute of limitations from one year to six months.

Corruption: The Anti-Corruption Commission is the main body responsible for combating corruption, although the Anti-Money Laundering Unit in the Central Bank is responsible for combating money laundering. Despite increased investigations, some local observers questioned the commission's effectiveness due to its limited jurisdiction, insufficient staff, legal obstacles, and the small number of investigations involving senior officials or large government projects. There were credible allegations that the commission failed to investigate cases involving high-level government officials.

The Ombudsman Bureau receives and investigates public complaints about corruption and misconduct by public officials.

There were no high-profile corruption convictions during the year. The commission received 1,072 complaints about corruption in 2015. It opened investigations into 460 cases, sent 63 to the PSD investigative liaison assigned to the commission, and six cases to the seconded prosecutor. The commission's investigations resulted in 13 convictions in 2015. Its annual report does not provide details of the cases. The Ombudsman Bureau received 638 complaints in 2015 and accepted 423 for investigation.

The Anti-Corruption Commission's prosecutor general levied charges in 66 corruption cases in 2015: 36 cases in the public sector and 30 in the private sector. Charges included embezzlement, fraud, forgery, bribery, wasting public funds, theft, failure to carry out job duties, lack of jurisdiction, and use of a stamp of a general directorate.

In September an online news site and Radio al-Balad published an investigation alleging that companies owned by relatives of several former members of parliament won millions of dollars in government tenders while they were in parliament.

Financial Disclosure: The law requires certain government officials (along with their spouses and dependent children) to declare their assets privately within three months of their assuming a government position. Officials rarely declared their assets. In the event of a complaint, the chief justice may review the disclosures. Under the law failure to disclose assets could result in a prison sentence of one week to three years or a fine of 5 to 200 JD ($7 to $280). As of September no officials were punished for failing to submit a disclosure.

Public Access to Information: The law provides for public access to government information that is a matter of legal record but denies requests for reasons of national security, public interest, and personal freedoms. The government has 30 days to respond to requests for information. If a government official refuses to respond to a request, the requester can appeal to the governmental Information

Council the decisions of which are nonbinding. The fees were not prohibitive and usually were associated with photocopy costs, if necessary. Journalists criticized the law, claiming that it permitted the government to deny requests without justification, or to refuse to respond, effectively denying the request.

Section 5. Governmental Attitude Regarding International and Nongovernmental Investigation of Alleged Violations of Human Rights

A number of domestic and international human rights groups operated in the country with some restrictions. The law gives the government the ability to control NGOs' internal affairs, including acceptance of foreign funding. NGOs generally were able to investigate and report publicly on human rights abuses throughout the year, although government officials were not always cooperative.

Government Human Rights Bodies: The National Center for Human Rights (NCHR) received both government and international funding. The prime minister nominates its board of trustees and then the king ratifies their appointment by royal decree. The government appoints NCHR's commissioner general. The NCHR produces an annual report on domestic human rights that sometimes criticizes government practices. NCHR recommendations are not legally binding, and the government often ignores them. In February the prime minister established a permanent governmental committee headed by the national human rights coordinator to review NCHR recommendations, as well as progress towards implementing international human rights commitments. On March 19, the government launched a 10-year comprehensive national human rights action plan designed to bring the law in line with international standards and best practices. Ministries formed working groups for implementation and published the plan on their websites. Additionally, the National Human Rights Coordinator collaborated with and increased communication among government ministries, governmental and nongovernmental organizations, media, and the international community on human rights problems. The Office of the National Human Rights Coordinator published a semiannual report on the government's progress regarding human rights on May 23. The National Human Rights Coordinator arranged semiannual meetings between government ministers, officials, and nongovernmental organizations.

Section 6. Discrimination, Societal Abuses, and Trafficking in Persons

Women

<u>Rape and Domestic Violence</u>: The law stipulates a sentence of at least 10 years of imprisonment with hard labor for the rape of a girl or woman 15 years of age or older. Spousal rape is not illegal. The Family Protection Law prescribes penalties of up to six months in prison for domestic abuse, but NGOs reported that judges rarely prosecuted cases under the Family Protection Law because judges considered its procedures unclear. Instead, they prosecuted domestic abuses cases under the penal code, as injury or sexual assault cases.

The government did not effectively enforce the law against rape, and violence and abuse against women was widespread. Women's rights activists speculated that many incidents went unreported because violence against women remained a taboo subject due to societal and familial pressures. The PSD's Family Protection Department reported 1,563 cases of domestic abuse as of September 30. Human rights activists stated that girls and women with disabilities were particularly at risk of gender-based violence.

Women may file complaints of rape or physical abuse with certain NGOs or directly with judicial authorities. As of September 30, the Family Protection Department treated and investigated 281 cases of rape or sexual assault against women. The Family Protection Department (FPD) actively investigated cases, but there were some reports of pressure on families to settle disputes via mediation instead of in the courts. NGOs reported that families often settled domestic abuse cases outside of the courts by requiring the abuser to sign before the governor or the FPD a statement promising not to reoffend. Spousal abuse is technically grounds for divorce, but husbands claimed religious authority to strike their wives. Observers noted that, while judges generally supported a woman's claim of abuse in court, due to societal and familial pressure, as well as fears of violence such as honor killings, few women sought legal remedies.

On May 4, the government launched a National Framework on Family Protection to enhance coordination, improve the referral mechanism, and identify roles and responsibilities for service providers combatting family violence. Observers believed the framework was an improvement from the previous framework, but also pointed out the continued need to amend the Family Protection Law. The prime minister issued a circular on May 4 instructing the government to start implementing the framework.

The Family Protection Department continued to operate a domestic violence hotline and received inquiries and complaints via the internet and e-mail. The prosecutor general seconded a criminal prosecutor to the Family Protection

Department headquarters so victims did not need go to the courts to file a criminal complaint. The department provided public information and training for government employees, including police, on domestic violence and rape. As of August 31, the government-run shelter Dar al-Wifaq al-Usari in Amman assisted 228 female victims of domestic violence and 58 children, according to the Ministry of Social Development. The government opened a second shelter for female victims of domestic violence in Irbid in October 2015. As of August 31, it had assisted 106 female victims of domestic violence and 34 children, according to the Ministry of Social Development. It provided reconciliation services to victims and their families and worked with NGOs to provide services, such as legal and medical assistance, as well as some vocational training. Observers noted the lack of a comprehensive approach for victims, such as psychosocial assistance.

The government-run center for trafficking victims in Amman, Dar al-Karamah, assisted 47 female victims of trafficking through September 30.

The government-run center for at-risk girls, Dar al-Khansa Juvenile Center, worked with NGOs to provide vocational training, education, and psychosocial assistance to minor female victims. As of November 1, the center had cared for 55 survivors of domestic violence or sexual abuse during the year, many of whom were at risk of additional violence from family members. It provided reconciliation services to victims and their families. Victims could only depart the shelter if a judge deemed reconciliation successful or if they transferred to another shelter at age 18.

Other Harmful Traditional Practices: The Ministry of Justice indicated that authorities referred four so-called "honor crimes" to the judicial system through September 29, with all four cases remaining under investigation, while NGOs reported 18 potential honor crimes through September. Activists reported that many such crimes went unreported. The Supreme Criminal Court's panel of judges dedicated to cases involving honor crimes in recent years routinely imposed prison sentences of up to 15 years to perpetrators of such crimes. The Cassation Court, which reviews the Supreme Criminal Court rulings, generally decreased the sentences by half. The Supreme Criminal Court issued one ruling on an honor crimes case during the year, sentencing a father to one year in prison for killing his daughter.

Generally, when the victim's family chose not to pursue the case, the government completely dismissed proceedings. In "honor crime" cases, the family of the victim and the family of the alleged perpetrator were often the same, since the perpetrator and victim usually were related. There were no reported instances of forced marriage as an alternative to a potential honor killing during the year, although NGOs noted that many cases of forced marriage occur shortly after an accusation of rape due to family and societal pressure before any formal trial begins. The penal code waives punishment for a rapist if he legally marries the victim and stays married for five years. Observers noted that if a woman marries her rapist, according to customary belief, her family members do not need to kill her to "preserve the family's honor."

On April 7, the prosecutor general detained a man in Irbid for further investigation related to the murder of his 16-year old sister in an apparent honor crime.

On April 27, the Supreme Criminal Court sentenced a father to one year in prison for killing his daughter in May 2015. The convicted man said he suspected his daughter had a romantic relationship outside of marriage, according to government officials and media reports. The case was pending with the Cassation Court. Through their administrative detention authority, governors continued to place potential victims of honor crimes in involuntary protective custody in the Women's Correctional and Rehabilitation Center in Jweideh detention facility and Umm al-Lulu detention facility, where some women remained for more than one year. The Family Protection Department has a liaison officer at Jweideh detention facility. Authorities held minor female victims of domestic violence or sexual abuse under unclear legal status at the Dar al-Khansa Juvenile Center. Authorities can release a woman detained in protective custody only after her family signs a statement assuring her safety, and both the local governor and the woman agree to the release. One NGO continued to work for the release of these women through mediation with their families. The NGO also provided a temporary but unofficial shelter for such women as an alternative to protective custody and provided post-release rehabilitation and job placement assistance.

Sexual Harassment: The law strictly prohibits sexual harassment and does not distinguish between sexual assault and sexual harassment. Both carry a minimum prison sentence of four years at hard labor. The government did not enforce this law. Women's groups stated that harassment was common, but many victims hesitated to file a complaint and rarely did so because they feared blame for inciting the harassment or consequences such as losing their job, or because they faced social and cultural pressure to remain silent. NGOs reported that refugees from Syria and foreign migrant workers, including garment workers and domestic workers, were especially vulnerable to gender-based violence, including sexual harassment and sexual assault, in the workplace.

<u>Reproductive Rights</u>: Couples have the basic right to decide the number, spacing, and timing of their children; manage their reproductive health; and individuals were able to make such decisions free from discrimination and coercion. Contraceptives were generally accessible to all men and women, both married and single, and provided free of charge in public clinics. According to estimates in the UN Population Fund's *State of World Population 2015*, 43 percent of women used a modern method of contraceptive, and 12 percent of women had an unmet need for family planning. Comprehensive essential obstetric, prenatal, and postnatal care was provided throughout the country in the public and private sectors.

<u>Discrimination</u>: The law does not provide for the same legal status and rights for women as for men. Women experienced discrimination in a number of areas, including inheritance, divorce, child custody, citizenship, pension and social security benefits, the workplace, and, in certain circumstances, the value of their testimony in a sharia court. In 2013, women owned only 20 percent of land and 25 percent of property, according to the Department of Statistics.

No specialized government office or designated official handles discrimination claims. The Jordanian National Commission for Women, a government-supported NGO, operated a hotline to receive discrimination complaints.

Under sharia law as applied in the country, female heirs receive half the amount that male heirs receive. A sole female heir receives only half of her parents' estate, with the balance going to designated male relatives, whereas a sole male heir inherits all of his parents' property. Women may seek divorce without the consent of their husbands in limited circumstances such as abandonment, spousal abuse, or in return for waiving financial rights. The law allows retention of financial rights under specific circumstances, such as spousal abuse. Special courts for each Christian denomination adjudicate marriage and divorce.

The law allows fathers to prevent their children under the age of 18 from leaving the country through a court order that is not available to mothers. Authorities did not stop fathers from exiting the country with their children when the mother objected.

The government provided men with more generous social security benefits than women. The government continued pension payments of deceased male civil servants to their heirs, but it discontinued payments to heirs of deceased female civil servants unless they were the sole income earner in the family. Laws and regulations governing health insurance for civil servants under the Civil Service Bureau do not permit married women to extend their health insurance coverage to dependents or spouses unless they are the sole income earner in the family. Divorced and widowed women may extend coverage to their children (see section 2.d., Stateless Persons, and section 7.d.).

Children

Birth Registration: Only the father transmits citizenship. The government did not issue birth certificates to all children born in the country during the year. The government deemed some children--including children of unmarried women, orphans, or of certain interfaith marriages involving a Muslim woman and converts from Islam to another religion--illegitimate and denied them proper registration, making it difficult or impossible for them to attend school, access health services, or receive other documentation. Illegitimate and abandoned children already holding national identity numbers have identity cards that clearly marked them as different; such numbers impeded these children as adults from obtaining employment, housing, and government benefits.

Education: Education is compulsory from ages six through 16 and free until age 18. No legislation exists to enforce the law or to punish guardians for violating it. Children without legal residency do not have the right to attend public school. The Ministry of Education allows Syrians to enroll at local public schools, with the exception of students who have been out of school for three or more years who authorities did not permit to register. In some cases, authorities did not permit refugee children to register in school due to lack of documentation. The UN Children's Fund (UNICEF) helped cover the cost and provided a supplement to Jordanian teachers who worked in Za'atri and Azraq camps and in the host communities. The government doubled the number of double-shift schools to allow an additional 50,000 Syrian refugee students access to formal education in addition to the 145,000 enrolled in 2015. Additionally, the UNRWA operated 172 primary schools for approximately 120,000 Palestinian refugee children and opened enrollment to Palestinian refugee children from Syria as well as a limited number of Syrian refugees residing in the Palestinian camps. Some children of female citizens and noncitizen fathers must apply for residency permits every year, and authorities did not assure permission (see section 2.d., Stateless Persons). Children with disabilities experienced extreme difficulty in accessing constitutionally protected early and primary education.

<u>Child Abuse</u>: The law specifies punishment for abuse of children. For example, conviction for rape of a child younger than age 15 potentially carries the death penalty. Local organizations working with abused children pointed to gaps in the legal system that regularly resulted in lenient sentencing, particularly for family members. For example, the penal code allows judges to reduce a sentence when the victim's family does not press charges. In child abuse cases, judges routinely showed leniency in accordance with the wishes of the family. As of September 30, authorities investigated 439 cases of child rape and sexual abuse.

The Juvenile Law places the age of criminal responsibility at 12 years. The law stipulates that juveniles charged with committing a crime along with an adult be tried in a juvenile court, except for crimes that fall under the jurisdiction of the State Security Court, such as terrorism charges, drug charges, or other charges relating to national security. During the year the government trained and assigned judges, prosecutors, and social workers to the juvenile court, although local legal aid organizations noted the court was still understaffed. The State Security Court issued a judgment that it does not have jurisdiction over juveniles. Terrorism-related trials of juveniles took place during the year in front of the juvenile criminal court. The 2016 Narcotics Law again gives the State Security Court jurisdiction over all drug-related criminal offenders, including juveniles. The new law stipulates alternative penalties for juvenile offenders, including vocational training and community service. Police stations have no designated holding areas for juveniles.

The government continued to fund a child protection center that provided temporary shelter and medical care for abused children between the ages of six and 12. Through September the shelter housed 41 abused children.

<u>Early and Forced Marriage</u>: The minimum age for marriage is 18. With the consent of both a judge and a guardian, a child as young as 15 years old, in most cases a girl, may be married. Several government sources estimated the rate of early marriage at 13 percent. In August, the Ministry of Justice reported that the rate of early marriage among Syrian girls was 35 percent, up from 32 percent reported in 2014. According to this year's census, 3.7 percent of girls in the country between the ages of 13 and 18 were married. There was no data available on the number of unregistered marriages, but it was likely that many Syrian refugee early marriages were not registered.

<u>Sexual Exploitation of Children</u>: The law stipulates a penalty for the commercial exploitation of children of six months' to three years' imprisonment. The law also

penalizes individuals who subject persons to trafficking for the purpose of sexual exploitation with a maximum of 10 years of hard labor and a fine of 2,000 to 50,000 JD ($2,800 to $70,000). The law prohibits the distribution of pornography involving persons under the age of 18 and provides for a fine of 300 JD to 5,000 JD ($420 to $7,000) or at least three months' imprisonment. The law does not specifically prohibit the possession of child pornography without an attention to sell or distribute. The law penalizes those who use the internet to post or distribute child pornography with a fine of 500 to 5,000 JD ($700 to $7,000) or at least six months' imprisonment. The minimum age of consensual sex is 18, although sexual relations between minors whose marriages the courts approved are legal.

Institutionalized Children: NGOs reported physical and sexual abuses occurred in government institutions. According to the NCHR, some juveniles in detention alleged mistreatment. Authorities automatically referred cases involving violence against persons with disabilities or institutionalized persons to the Family Protection Department. The community monitoring committee highlighted the pervasive use of physical discipline, physical and verbal abuse, unacceptable living conditions, and a lack of educational, rehabilitative, or psychosocial services for wards and inmates. NGOs noted that the Ministry of Social Development was responsive and followed up on reports from the community monitoring committee. Activists for orphans' rights alleged that adult orphans and former wards of the state were especially vulnerable to forced and early marriage, labor trafficking, and sexual exploitation.

International Child Abductions: The country is not a party to the 1980 Hague Convention on the Civil Aspects of International Child Abduction. See the Department of State's *Annual Report on International Parent Child Abduction* at travel.state.gov/content/childabduction/en/legal/compliance.html.

Anti-Semitism

Aside from foreigners, there was no resident Jewish community in the country. Anti-Semitism was present in media. Editorial cartoons, articles, and opinion pieces sometimes negatively depicted Jews without government response. The national school curriculum, including materials on tolerance education, did not include mention of the Holocaust.

Trafficking in Persons

See the Department of State's *Trafficking in Persons Report* at
www.state.gov/j/tip/rls/tiprpt/.

Persons with Disabilities

The law generally provides equal rights to persons with disabilities, but authorities did not uphold such legal protections. Disabilities covered under the law include physical, sensory, psychological, and mental disabilities. Activists noted the law on the rights of persons with disabilities lacked implementing regulations. The Higher Council for Affairs of Persons with Disabilities, a government body, worked with ministries, the private sector, and NGOs to formulate and implement strategies to assist persons with disabilities. Citizens and NGOs universally reported that persons with disabilities faced problems in obtaining employment and accessing education, health care, transportation, and other services, particularly in rural areas.

The government's emergency call center has video-teleconference capability with sign-language interpretation available for persons with hearing disabilities. The PSD received 650 calls from persons with hearing disabilities through the beginning of September.

Human rights activists reported that institutions and rehabilitation centers subjected some persons with disabilities to negligence and cruel and inhuman treatment. On May 15, the Ministry of Social Development reported that it had withdrawn the operating license for one center for persons with disabilities for abuse, and since the beginning of the year had warned 15 other centers for violating rules and regulations.

The electoral law directs the government to verify that voting facilities are accessible to persons with disabilities and allows such persons to bring a personal assistant to the polling station; the Independent Electoral Commission has responsibility for implementing this law. Many polling stations visited by international observers during the September 20 parliamentary elections were not accessible to persons with disabilities as they were located up steps or on the higher floors of buildings. Polling center staff made efforts to assist voters. The Independent Electoral Commission allocated one polling center in each governorate to be accessible for the deaf and hearing-impaired. For the first time, the Higher Council for Affairs of Persons with Disabilities was part of election monitoring teams. The council trained 118 observers specifically to monitor for accessibility for persons with disabilities.

Banks frequently refused to allow persons with vision disabilities to open a bank account independently and required blind applicants to bring two male witnesses to certify each transaction. Banks commonly refused to issue customers with vision disabilities automated teller machine cards.

According to the Higher Council for Affairs of Persons with Disabilities and 2015 data, only 3 percent of children with disabilities enrolled in schools. The 2013 NCHR report noted that school classrooms were not fully accessible, and there were no qualified teachers for children with disabilities; these problems remained throughout the year. The council reported that educational accommodations were more readily available at the university level than in elementary and secondary schools. At all levels of education, authorities excluded children with certain types of disabilities from studying certain subjects and often could not access critical educational support services, such as sign-language interpretation. Authorities did not train general education teachers to work with students with various disabilities. Families of children with disabilities reported that teachers and principals often refused to include children with disabilities in mainstream classrooms. The Ministry of Education provided accessible transportation to specialized centers for children with disabilities, but not to mainstream schools. There remained insufficient capacity in specialized centers for all students who required accommodations. Students with significant intellectual disabilities fell under the authority of the Ministry of Social Development rather than the Ministry of Education.

The law tasks the Special Buildings Code Department with enforcing accessibility provisions and oversees retrofitting of existing buildings to comply with building codes. The vast majority of private and public office buildings continued to have limited or no access for persons with disabilities. Municipal infrastructure such as public transport, streets, sidewalks, and intersections was not accessible. A 2014 report by the Higher Council for Affairs of Persons with Disabilities, the Department of Statistics, and the Washington Group found that 76 percent of persons with disabilities over the age of 15 years were economically inactive.

The law mandates that public- and private-sector establishments with between 25 and 50 workers employ at least one person with disabilities and that establishments with more than 50 workers must reserve 4 percent of their positions for persons with disabilities. The law lacked implementing regulations, and authorities rarely enforced it. Additionally, authorities exempted employers who state the nature of the work is not suitable for persons with disabilities from the quota. Employers, including the government's Civil Service Bureau, frequently required potential employees with disabilities to present a medical letter certifying the bearer was competent to perform the job in question. Human rights activists considered the letter a significant barrier to participation in public life because some medical professionals were not aware of the full range of accommodations available and thus certified individuals as not able to perform certain tasks. Girls and women with disabilities were particularly at risk for gender-based violence.

Human rights activists and the media reported that children and adults with disabilities were vulnerable to physical and sexual abuse while in institutions, rehabilitation centers, or other care settings, including their family homes. The government operated some of these institutions, and some of the abusers were government employees. Media reported some instances of abuse of persons with disabilities by family members during the year; the government launched investigations into many of these cases and referred the victims for assistance.

The government provides tariff exemptions for the vehicles of persons with disabilities and reduces the costs of hiring domestic help for persons with disabilities. Approximately 10,000 persons with disabilities (some 17 percent of the total estimated population with disabilities) benefited from these measures in 2015.

National/Racial/Ethnic Minorities

Four groups of Palestinians resided in the country, many of whom faced some discrimination. Those who migrated to the country and the Jordan-controlled West Bank after the 1948 Arab-Israeli war received full citizenship, as did those who migrated to the country after the 1967 war and held no residency entitlement in the West Bank. Those still holding residency in the West Bank after 1967 were no longer eligible to claim full citizenship but could obtain temporary travel documents without national identification numbers, provided they did not also carry a Palestinian Authority travel document. These individuals had access to some government services but paid noncitizen rates at hospitals, educational institutions, and training centers. Refugees who fled Gaza after 1967 were not entitled to citizenship, and authorities issued them temporary travel documents without national numbers. These persons had no access to government services and were almost completely dependent on UNRWA services. Finally, Palestinian refugees from Syria who were able to enter the country, despite many being turned away at the border, had access to UNRWA services.

Palestinians were underrepresented in parliament and senior positions in the government and the military, as well as in admissions to public universities. They had limited access to university scholarships.

Acts of Violence, Discrimination, and Other Abuses Based on Sexual Orientation and Gender Identity

Authorities can arrest LGBTI individuals for violating public order or acting indecently in public, crimes under the penal code, although arrests were rare during the year. While consensual same-sex sexual conduct is not illegal, societal discrimination against LGBTI persons was prevalent, and LGBTI persons were targets of abuse. Activists reported discrimination in housing, employment, education, and access to public services. Some LGBTI individuals reported reluctance to engage the legal system due to fear their sexual orientation or gender identity would either provoke hostile reactions from police or disadvantage them in court. Activists reported that most LGBTI individuals were closeted and feared disclosure of their sexual identity.

During the year there were reports of individuals who left the country due to fear that their families would punish them because of their sexual orientation. There were also credible reports that an LGBTI individual was the victim of an "honor crime."

HIV and AIDS Social Stigma

HIV/AIDS was a largely taboo subject. Lack of public awareness remained a problem, because many citizens believed the disease exclusively affected foreigners and members of the LGBTI community. Society stigmatized HIV/AIDS-positive individuals, and they largely hid their medical status. The government continued its efforts to inform the public about the disease and eliminate negative attitudes about persons with HIV/AIDS, but it also continued to test all foreigners annually for HIV/AIDS, hepatitis B, syphilis, malaria, and tuberculosis. The government deported individuals who tested HIV-positive.

Section 7. Worker Rights

a. Freedom of Association and the Right to Collective Bargaining

The law, including related regulations and statutes, provides for the right to form and join free trade unions and conduct legal strikes, but with significant restrictions. There is no right to collective bargaining, although the labor code provides for collective agreements. The law identifies specific groups of public- and private-sector workers who may organize and defines 17 industries and professions in which trade unions may be established. The establishment of new unions requires approval from the Ministry of Labor and at least 50 founding members. The law requires that these 17 trade unions belong to the government-subsidized General Federation of Jordanian Trade Unions, the country's sole trade union federation. The law authorizes additional professions on a case-by-case basis to form professional associations. Authorities do not permit civil servants to form or join unions, and they cannot engage in collective bargaining. The constitution prohibits antiunion discrimination, and the law protects workers from employer retaliation due to union affiliation or activities. The law does not explicitly provide a worker fired due to antiunion views with the right to reinstatement.

Regulations refer conflicts during negotiations first to a mediator appointed by the Ministry of Labor. If the case is unresolved, it moves to the minister of labor and then to a mediation council composed of an employee representative, a labor representative, and a chair appointed by the minister of labor. The minister refers conflicts not settled by the council to a labor court with a panel of ministry-appointed judges. There are limits on the right to strike, including a requirement to provide a minimum of 14 days' notice to the employer. The law prohibits strikes if a labor dispute is under mediation or arbitration.

The law allows foreign workers to join unions, but it does not permit them to create unions, head a union, or hold union office. In at least one sector, elections for the union board may have excluded some migrant workers from voting for their leaders because it was unclear whether they could vote for offices they could not hold. It remained unclear whether the law permits domestic and agricultural workers to create or join unions or whether the labor code grants them other protections. Labor court judges were divided over whether the entire labor code applied to domestic workers or whether only a specific regulation for domestic workers, cooks, gardeners, and similar workers applied. The government did not fully enforce applicable laws with effective remedies, and penalties were insufficient to deter violations.

The government did not fully respect freedom of association and the right to collective bargaining. Many worker organizations were not independent of the government, and government influence on union policies and activities continued.

The government subsidized and audited salaries and activities of the General Federation of Jordanian Trade Unions and monitored union elections. The government denied recognition to independent unions organized outside the structure of the government-approved federation. The government did not meet with these unions, and the lack of legal recognition often hampered their ability to collect dues, obtain meeting space, and otherwise address members' workplace concerns. The General Federation of Jordanian Trade Unions also reported trouble getting government recognition for trade unions in new sectors beyond the 17 established in law.

As of September 18, the Ministry of Labor reported 35 strikes and labor protests. There were no reports of threats of violence against union heads, although labor activists alleged that the security services pressured union leaders to refrain from activism that challenged government interests. Strikes generally occurred without advance notice or registration.

Labor organizations reported that management representatives used threats to intimidate striking workers. Labor organizations and industry representatives reported that workers also sometimes used threats and physical violence to retaliate against management officials or to coerce colleagues into participating in labor actions.

Foreign workers in the garment, construction, services, and agricultural sectors, whose residency permits are tied to work contracts, were vulnerable to retaliation by employers for participating in strikes and sit-ins. Participation in a legally unrecognized strike counted as an unexcused absence for the purpose of this law. The law allows employers to consider employment contracts void if a worker is absent more than 10 consecutive days, as long as the employer provides written notice. The Ministry of Labor sometimes prevented management from arbitrarily dismissing foreign workers engaged in labor or other activism, but its enforcement was inconsistent. Observers reported management's common practice of refusing to renew foreign workers' contracts due to "troublemaking" or attempting to organize in the workplace.

As of November 21, the Ministry of Labor received 3,176 labor complaints and settled 241 during the year.

While the Ministry of Labor received no complaints of antiunion discrimination during the year, observers noted that the labor code did not explicitly protect nonunionized workers from retaliation. This was particularly the case for foreign workers in all sectors as well as citizens working in the public sector on short-term contracts (day laborers).

Labor NGOs working to promote the rights of workers generally focused on promoting the rights of migrant workers. NGOs did not face additional or different government restrictions than those discussed in section 2.b.

b. Prohibition of Forced or Compulsory Labor

The law prohibits all forms of forced or compulsory labor except in a state of emergency, such as war or natural disaster. The government made substantial efforts to enforce the law through inspections and other means. Labor activists noted that law enforcement and judicial officials did not consistently identify victims or open criminal investigations.

Police investigated and referred 28 cases of forced labor involving 54 potential victims to the prosecutor general as trafficking cases in 2015. In 2015 the Joint Anti-Trafficking Unit of the Public Security Directorate investigated 178 cases of nonpayment of wages, withholding of passports, breaches of contracts, inappropriate work conditions, and prolonged hours without overtime pay. Police referred 124 potential victims of forced labor to shelter services. In 2015 the Ministry of Justice recorded 13 convictions under the trafficking in persons law.

In the garment sector, the government inspected factories and investigated allegations of forced labor. According to NGOs reports of withholding passports continued to decline during the year, particularly those of workers in the garment sector. Forced labor or conditions indicative of forced labor occurred, particularly among migrant workers in the domestic work and agricultural sectors. Activists highlighted the vulnerability of agricultural workers due to minimal government oversight. Activists also identified domestic workers as particularly vulnerable to exploitation due to inadequate government oversight, social norms that excused forced labor, and workers' isolation within individual homes. Labor inspectors did not regularly investigate reports of labor or other abuses of domestic workers in private homes, and inspectors could not enter a private residence without the owner's permission except with a court order. NGOs and foreign embassy representatives reported the Joint Anti-Trafficking Unit preferred to settle potential cases of domestic servitude through mediation, rather than referring them for criminal prosecution.

The government continued its cooperation with foreign embassies to waive overstay fees for migrant domestic workers who wish to repatriate after a two-year stay in the country. The government also has a liaison officer permanently based at the international airport to facilitate voluntary repatriation of trafficking victims.

Government bylaws require recruitment agencies for migrant domestic workers to provide health insurance, workplace accident insurance, and insurance that reimburses the recruitment fees to employers when a worker leaves before fulfilling her contract. If the employer fails to pay the worker's salary or return the worker's passport, then the employer would not be entitled to the insurance payment. The bylaws give the Ministry of Labor the authority publicly to classify recruitment agencies based on compliance, and to close and withdraw the license of poorly ranked agencies. Under the bylaws the ministry closed seven recruitment agencies and temporarily suspended 18 agencies as of September; most had been the subject of repeated complaints.

Also see the Department of State's *Trafficking in Persons Report* at www.state.gov/j/tip/rls/tiprpt/.

c. Prohibition of Child Labor and Minimum Age for Employment

The law forbids employment of children younger than 16 years of age, except as apprentices in nonhazardous positions. The law bans those between the ages of 16 and 18 from working in potentially hazardous jobs, limits working hours for such children to six hours per day, mandates one-hour breaks for every four consecutive working hours, and prohibits work after 8 p.m. on national or religious holidays and on weekends.

There were instances of child labor, and many local and international organizations reported it was on the rise, particularly among the Syrian refugee community. Children worked in wholesale, retail, manufacturing, mechanical repair, agriculture, construction, quarrying, tour-guiding, and the hotel and restaurant industry. They also worked as street vendors, carpenters, blacksmiths, domestic workers, and painters, as well as in small family businesses. The Ministry of Labor reported that children faced occupation-specific hazards in employment that involved mechanical work and welding, where they often lacked the training and protective equipment to perform work safely. The Center for Strategic Studies at the University of Jordan, in collaboration with the International Labor Organization, the Labor Ministry, and the Department of Statistics, published the summary report of a national child labor survey in August. The survey showed that an estimated 76,000 children between the ages of five and 17 were working in the country, and that 44,000 of them were working in dangerous jobs. Approximately 1.9 percent of the four million children of all nationalities residing in the country were employed.

The Labor Ministry's three-person Child Labor Unit was responsible for coordinating government action regarding child labor and, with the department's labor inspectors, was responsible for enforcing all aspects of the labor code, including child labor. Through September 18, the ministry reported that labor inspectors found 1,271 child laborers (955 Jordanians and 316 Syrians), and issued 671 warnings and 1,007 violations. Authorities referred violators to an administrative labor court; the Ministry of Justice had no information on any child labor cases referred to criminal courts. The law provides that employers who hired a child younger than age 16 pay a fine of as much as 500 JD ($700), which doubles for repeat offenses.

Labor inspectors reportedly attempted alternative approaches before issuing official warnings and violations, such as issuing advice and guidance, ensuring safe work conditions, and cooperating with employers to permit working children to attend school concurrently.

The government's capacity to implement and enforce child labor laws was not sufficient to deter violations. The government lacked capacity to monitor children working in the informal work sector such as children working in family businesses and the agricultural sector.

The Ministries of Labor, Education, and Social Development collaborated with NGOs aiming to withdraw children from the worst forms of labor.

According to a report by UNICEF and Save the Children, close to one-half of all Syrian refugee children in Jordan were the joint or sole family breadwinners with most of them involved in armed conflict, sexual exploitation, and illicit activities, including organized begging and child trafficking. Syrian refugee children worked in the informal sector without legal work permits. Syrian refugee children sold goods in the streets in many parts of the country and begged in urban areas.

Also, see the Department of Labor's *Findings on the Worst Forms of Child Labor* at www.dol.gov/ilab/reports/child-labor/findings/.

d. Discrimination with Respect to Employment and Occupation

Labor laws do not prohibit discrimination with respect to employment and occupation on the basis of race, sex, gender, disability, language, political opinion, national origin or citizenship, age, sexual orientation and/or gender identity, HIV-positive status or other communicable diseases, or social status.

Discrimination in employment and occupation occurred with respect to gender, disability, national origin, and sexual orientation (see section 6).

Union officials reported that sectors employing predominantly women, such as secretarial work, offered wages below the official minimum wage of 190 JD ($266) per month. On August 24, news outlets published a report that the Social Security Corporation had identified 1,500 women doing secretarial work earning under the minimum wage. Many women said traditional social pressures discouraged them from pursuing professional careers, especially after marriage. According to the Jordanian National Commission for Women, one-half of the country's university graduates were women, but women comprised only 13 percent of the labor force.

Persons with disabilities faced discrimination in employment and access to the workplace. Migrant workers, faced discrimination in wages, housing, and working conditions (see section 7.e.).

e. Acceptable Conditions of Work

In 2012 the government raised the national minimum wage to 190 JD ($266) per month, and the poverty level was set at 366 JD ($512) per month for a family of five. According to the World Bank, nearly one-third of Jordanians were living below the poverty line at some point throughout the year. The minimum wage increase excluded noncitizens and all workers in the garment industry. Citizen workers in the garment industry received a minimum wage of 190 JD ($266) per month; noncitizen workers in the garment industry received a minimum wage of 110 JD ($154) per month, although many had base wages slightly above the minimum wage. Authorities granted this exemption in part because employers often provided room and board for noncitizen workers in this sector. Some garment factories continued to deduct room and board from foreign workers' already lower salaries.

The law sets a standard workweek of 48 hours and requires overtime pay for hours worked in excess of that standard. The law provides for 14 days of paid annual leave per year, which increases to 21 days after five years of service. Workers also received additional national and religious holidays designated by the government. Employees are entitled to one day off per week. The law permits compulsory overtime under certain circumstances such as conducting an annual inventory, closing accounts, preparing to sell goods at discounted prices, avoiding loss to goods that would otherwise be exposed to damage, and receiving special deliveries. In such cases actual working hours may not exceed 10 hours per day, the employee must be paid overtime, and the period may not last more than 30 days. There is no cap on the amount of consensual overtime.

The government set occupational health and safety standards. Employers are required to abide by all such standards set by the Ministry of Labor. The law requires employers to protect workers from hazards caused by the nature of the job or its tools, provide any necessary protective equipment, train workers on hazards and prevention measures, provide first aid as necessitated by the job, and protect employees from explosions or fires by storing flammable materials appropriately.

The Ministry of Labor is responsible for enforcement of labor laws and acceptable conditions of work. Ministry inspectors enforced the labor code but were unable to assure full compliance; there were 215 inspectors for the entire country, an insufficient number to enforce the labor code effectively. Employees may lodge complaints regarding violations of the labor code directly with the Ministry of Labor or through organizations such as their union or the NCHR. The ministry opened an investigation for each complaint.

Labor standards apply to the informal sector, but the Labor Ministry lacked the capacity to detect and monitor workplace violations. Authorities did not consistently apply all the protections of the labor code to domestic and agricultural workers, because their applicability was not clear. Labor contacts stated that agricultural and domestic workers, cooks, and gardeners were not entitled to social benefits from the Social Security Corporation.

The government took action to prevent violations and improve working conditions. As of September 18, the 215 labor inspectors conducted 60,617 inspections and issued 5,415 warnings and 4,621 violations nationwide. Labor inspectors warned 1,064 workplaces of closure and closed 516 for lack of compliance. The Labor Ministry placed a special focus on enforcing compliance in the Qualifying Industrial Zones, which largely employed migrant garment workers. The ratio of labor inspectors to workers or places of employment was significantly higher in these zones than for the general population. The government required export garment manufacturers to participate in the Better Work Jordan program to improve labor standards. As of September, 73 factories required by the government to join Better Work Jordan were active members of the program; four factories had yet to submit their registration.

Wage, overtime, safety, and other standards often were not upheld in several sectors, including construction, mechanic shops, day labor, and the garment industry. Some foreign workers faced hazardous and exploitative working conditions in a variety of sectors. Authorities did not effectively protect employees who attempted to remove themselves from situations that endangered their health and safety. Union leaders and the media reported that female citizen workers were more likely to encounter labor violations; including wages below the minimum wage and harassment in the workplace. According to Labor Ministry statistics, the gender gap in wages in the private sector was 41 percent, and 28 percent in the public sector.

Because there was no limit on consensual overtime, the Labor Ministry permitted employees in some industries, such as the garment sector, to work excessive workweeks, reportedly as much as 80 to 100 hours per week.

In the garment sector, foreign workers were more susceptible than their citizen counterparts to dangerous or unfair conditions, including mandatory overtime, delayed payment of wages, deductions for room and board, and unacceptable dormitory conditions. As of September the Labor Ministry closed 418 workplaces for recruiting foreign workers without work permits. Better Work Jordan found that compliance regarding coercion improved. Indebtedness of migrant garment workers to third parties and involuntary or excessive overtime persisted.

Employers subjected some workers in the agricultural sector, the vast majority of whom were Egyptians, to exploitative conditions. According to a domestic NGO, agricultural workers usually received less than the minimum wage, worked excessive hours without adequate compensation, and lived in substandard housing. Some employers in the agricultural sector also reportedly confiscated passports. Egyptian migrant workers were also vulnerable to exploitation in the construction industry; employers usually paid them less than the minimum wage, and they lacked basic training and equipment necessary to uphold occupational health and safety standards.

Domestic workers, overwhelmingly migrants, often faced unacceptable working conditions. Many domestic workers reported to local NGOs and their embassies that they received insufficient food, no private accommodations, no health care, no days off, and long delays in or nonpayment of wages. While domestic workers could file complaints in person with the Labor Ministry Domestic Workers Directorate or the PSD, many domestic workers complained there was no follow-up on their cases either from the ministry or from the PSD. Callers to a domestic-worker hotline of the Labor Ministry reported that live operators were available only during government business hours, or seven hours a day during the workweek. After-hours calls required the caller to leave a message and a callback number, which posed particular difficulties for domestic workers who had access only to their employers' telephones. Advocates for migrant workers reported that hotline instructions in Arabic were difficult for noncitizens to understand and that some key languages were still missing from the hotline translation service.

In August 2015 the prosecutor general charged a Jordanian woman in Irbid with premeditated murder after she allegedly beat an Indonesian domestic worker in her employ to death. The victim died in October 2015, and the forensic report showed that the worker died due to brain hemorrhage. The case was pending at year's end.

Advocates for migrant domestic workers reported that domestic workers who sought government assistance or made allegations against their employers frequently faced counterclaims of criminal behavior from their employers. Employers could file criminal complaints or flight notifications against domestic workers with police stations. Even when domestic workers benefited from initiatives such as the general amnesty that waived immigration overstay fines, such alerts on file with police could prevent them from leaving the country.

During the year dozens of domestic workers from the Philippines, Indonesia, and Sri Lanka sought shelter at their countries' embassies in Amman. The government-run shelter for victims of trafficking assisted 47 women victims of trafficking through September 30, including workers from Bangladesh and the Philippines. Most of the domestic workers reportedly fled conditions indicative of forced labor or abuse, including unpaid wages and, to a lesser extent, sexual or physical abuse. By law employers are responsible for renewing foreign employees' residency permits but often failed to do so for domestic employees. As a result authorities considered most of the domestic workers sheltered by embassies illegal residents, and many were stranded because they were unable to pay the daily overstay fees of 1.50 JD ($2.10) to depart the country. The government continued its cooperation with foreign embassies to waive overstay fees for migrant domestic workers who wished to repatriate after a two-year stay in the country, a policy that has been in place since 2013 and greatly reduced the number of domestic workers stranded at their embassies' shelters.

As a result of poor working conditions experienced by some of its citizens, Indonesia prohibited its citizens from traveling to Jordan as domestic workers. Some human rights organizations argued that these bans heightened the vulnerability of foreign domestic workers who turned to unscrupulous recruitment agencies to migrate illegally to the country.